funfacts about Betta Fish

37 Frequently Asked Questions by Betta Pet Owners & Lovers

Short Picture Book for Kids

BY FIONA WEBER

All rights reserved
© Fiona Weber | The World of Rare Pets
No part of this publication may be reproduced, distributed or transmitted without prior written permission of the publisher.

Introduction

What about keeping an aquarium not so big and not so small, with a beautiful natural decoration and a fish that is so colorful that it takes your breath away? If that's what you're after, Betta fish might be the perfect addition.

In addition to being a very easy-to-keep species, those fish are full of character and personality. One of the best attributes is that Bettas are available in virtually any color, pattern, and type of fins. No wonder why it is one of the most popular fish available worldwide.

Even with all the ease of having one of these fish, you may still need to find out whether they are a good choice to keep as a pet. We made this exclusive ebook to solve your doubts, answering all common questions about Betta fish.

1. Where is Betta fish found?

The Betta fish, aka Siamese Fighting Fish (Betta splendens), is a fish of the Anabantidae family (same family as the gouramis). Betta splendens is a species native to Southeast Asia. In nature, these fish live in places with generally dark water and with slow flow or even standing water, such as temporary ponds and flooded river banks. They are also prevalent in rice fields when these fields are flooded. In its habitat, you can find a lot of submerged vegetation. This vegetation is essential to species that live there, as Bettas use it to hide and camouflage themselves against predators.

Wild fish are small and dull brown or green in color, unlike domesticated strains.

2. Is my Betta a tropical fish species?

For sure, and beyond that, the Betta is probably one of the most famous tropical fish in the world! Tropical fish occur in places with warm temperatures, so they must be kept in heated aquariums. Generally, these species need higher temperatures, ranging between 77 and 86 F. Fish in this category are much more prevalent in the aquarium and are easy to find in pet stores.

3. How long does Betta fish live?

Bettas generally live 3 to 5 years in captivity. The lifespan of your Betta fish depends directly on the quality of life you offer the animal, such as the size and composition of the aquarium, food, and water maintenance. Your fish can even live up to five years if it has enough space, with a

quality filter, heating, and a balanced diet.

4. What are the different types and breeds of Betta?

As mentioned earlier, wild bettas were different from those bred today. Wild fish are also much smaller than domesticated ones. It is believed that at the time of the Plakat collections in Siam, breeders identified animals with larger fins. They would separate these animals as they thought they were not efficient concerning other fish. As a result, they were slower and tired faster, in addition to being less aggressive.

Bettas arrived in Europe in mid-1896 in Germany and from 1910 in the United States.

In 1967, the IBC (International Betta Congress), founded by Dr. Gene Lucas to research and develop Betta fish, set several research lines to determine bettas' genetic traceability.

Bettas are one of the most bred fish in the world, so they are available in many different shapes and cores, each type having its name.

With more and more varieties being endlessly produced, many hobbyists, even the most experienced, need clarification on the names and what they stand for.

A Betta's colors are formed in layers; to produce a specific color, other layered shades must first be "taken off" through selective breeding.

Breeding fish to obtain unique and desired traits requires knowledge of the genetic load (lineage) that both parents carry.

On the other hand, raising males as ornamental fish for sale and export is becoming increasingly profitable in the market.

5. What is the rarest Betta type?

The rarity of a Betta fish depends on a few factors: the type of fins and the fish's color.

Fish with the "Fantail" fin-type (a fan-shaped double tail) are considered rare, as it is a purely recessive trait.

Bettas with the perfect round tail are also rare and hard to find.

As for the color, the ones at the top of the list of the rarest found in these fish would be the ones called "Purple" and "Pink."

6. Why is Betta fish called fighting fish?

The name Fighting fish was given because the local population uses the fish for fights. Due to the aggressiveness and territoriality of the males, when placed in the same place, these fish will fight incessantly. Because of this factor, the population of some Asian countries uses them for competitive fights.

There are countless differences in the fighting lineage from the other bloodlines. Fighting fish are selected for different characteristics besides color, so they usually have colors similar to wild fish. Fish bred for the fight are selected to have robust bodies featuring hard scales and smaller fins as protection against the opponent's attacks.

In this type of lineage, colors and patterns are

not necessary. Instead, the predisposition to the ability to attack vulnerable targets, such as fins and the tail, is an essential resource.

Reports from scholars and Betta lovers date back more than 170 years to discovering this beautiful animal in its natural habitat.

Thai people already used bettas in fights, and with high stakes in value, they bet everything they had.

7. Are Bettas good pets?

Yes, for sure, if they weren't, they wouldn't have been kept and bred with such dedication for more than 170 years. They are incredibly resistant fish that adapt to different environments and extreme living conditions. Therefore, the temperature is the only limiting factor for keeping them in captivity.

8. Are Betta fish easy to care for?

It is undoubtedly one of the easiest fish to have at home.

In addition to being easy to care for, betta fish are adaptable, so they do well in different aquariums. However, the tank's space must not be too small; it must provide enough room for the fish to feel safe and to have a heating and filtration system.

9. What is the normal behavior of Betta Fish?

There are behavioral differences concerning the sex of these fish.

The aggressive behavior in male Bettas is mainly because it is a very territorial species. Therefore, their aggression usually occurs with similar-looking fish.

When kept under ideal conditions, Bettas are great fish for community aquariums. But they can become more aggressive when stressed or uncomfortable, attacking different fish and trying to

jump out of the aquarium at all costs.

Betta fish can be active fish and very passive at the same time.

Bettas like to swim through the entire water column, play, and hide in underwater vegetation and among the decor. They are super curious and intelligent fish, hiding only when they feel threatened or something is wrong. Females inherited the same aggressive genes as males. However, they tend to be much more sociable and friendly. As a result, many aquarists maintain aquariums with several females together. Although there is always some fight here and there, females can still live peacefully together. On the other hand, when males are kept together, they often end up with gnawed fins or dead fish unless you set up giant tanks with lots of hiding places.

10. Do Betta fishes recognize their owners?

A great question! Most of the time, yes, they do. The Betta is a small fish and does not have the same intelligence as mammals. Still, we already know its intellectual capacity is enough to recognize a person and create a bond.

More specifically, a betta is smart enough to identify people and objects and make associations with particular patterns. Although the Betta brain does not have the same capacities for emotions as a dog's, a betta fish can sense and show its feelings.

Your betta fish will recognize you over time. It is a curious fish that likes interacting with objects inside and outside the aquarium. So whoever is feeding him will eventually be recognized by him. That's why it's interesting that the owner is the main person to feed him.

But remember, just as betta fish can recognize you and be happy to see you, they can also get scared and swim away if they don't associate you with good things. So remember that, just like with people, how you treat your Betta dictates your relationship with him.

11. Is my Betta fish nocturnal?

Not really; Bettas fish are diurnal animals. They stay awake during the day. Therefore, perform maintenance and feedings always during the day.

But be clear. These animals don't like bright lights in their tank; remember, only leave the aquarium lit for 8 hours.

12. Which type of Betta should I get?

The Betta strain does not make much difference in handling and care.

But try to start with the most common varieties of Betta. Choose a color and a type of fin that catches your eye, and make sure the fish is healthy.

13. Can my Betta bite me?
As a form of aggression, never.
They may bite your fingers and mistake them for food during feeding or jump on the food and hit your finger, but don't worry, it won't hurt you or your fish.

14. How do I entertain my betta fish?
Betta fish is a charming, intelligent fish and loves to play!
This fish is among the most intelligent freshwater fish species, learning many tricks and games. With the proper training, you'll be able to give your friend instructions and build stronger bonds with him!

Never touch or pet the Betta fish because they are very sensitive, and touching them can take some mucus protection from their scales.

But you can play with it with your fingers, placing one of them on the glass so the fish can follow it. Go from one side of the aquarium to the other and sometimes change the path.

You can also put your finger on the water's surface to make it come to you and thus practice jump.

Over the days, you can increase the height of the jump. However, it is essential not to exaggerate because the Betta can jump out of the aquarium!

Place a ball hanging or inside the aquarium to avoid leaving it without activity for a long time. It will make him curious. With that, he will spend hours swimming around or jumping.

Use a mirror in front of the aquarium or inside. When the Betta fish notices it, it will think it's another fish. With this, it will open the fins, an excellent enrichment exercise.

15. What do I need to keep a Betta fish healthy?

Before buying a Betta fish, ensure you have the means to keep it. We know that it requires much less attention and care than a dog or a cat, but like any living being, it cannot be neglected.

When assembling your Betta aquarium, it is essential to place some accessories to form a look closer to the natural environment and provide what the fish needs.

Opt for soft gravel or sand to place at the bottom of the aquarium; about 1 inch is enough. So remember to put driftwood, decorations, and rocks too.

Those decorations give the tank a more natural look and serve as a place for the inhabitants. Plants are welcome too.

Bettas must inhabit conventional aquariums, so you must always provide filtration and a heating system.

Bettas have difficulty swimming in strong currents, so try to choose a small, slow-flowing filter, such as a Hang-on or sponge filter.

In addition, you will need

a lamp to enjoy your fish during the day and control the circadian cycle. Remember that Bettas need light during the day and darkness at night to stay healthy.

Lastly, don't forget about water conditioners, commercial, live or frozen foods, and water tests.

16. What is the ideal size of my Betta fish tank?
Despite the Betta fish spending more time at the bottom of the aquarium, contrary to what many people say, it needs a particular space. Therefore, use an aquarium of at least 10 gallons for a Betta fish. Tiny aquariums can make the animal stressed.

If you want to keep Betta with other fish, the indication goes up to a minimum 20-gallon aquarium.

17. Can I use tap water for my Betta?
You must never use tap

water directly in the fish tank. Instead, you must always condition the water.

Water is the primordial environment for fish life and must be cared for with impeccable dedication.

In drinking water, elements such as chlorine are added to remove possible bacteria and other infective beings, thus making the water fit for our consumption. Fish are susceptible animals, so we must use products called water conditioners. These products will chemically remove harmful elements like chlorine and heavy metals.

Another point to be considered is the adjustment of the chemical characteristics of the water, such as pH, hardness, etc. For this, we do specific tests (you

can find them in aquarium stores) and adapt the water to the needs and values of your fish.

18. Which tankmates can I use with my Betta?
Some fish species can live along Bettas peacefully. As much as Bettas have been bred in aquariums throughout history, their strong fighting instinct has never been put aside. That's why some fish can be so territorial that they cannot coexist with other species in the same tank. At the same time, some fish are so calm that they can even be bothered by their tankmates.
In this way, we realize that each fish is unique, having its personality.

Always remember the aggressiveness of male fish, so you should never put more than one male in an aquarium and never mix males and females.

Female Bettas can live in a group without too many problems Corydoras, Oto Catfish, Apistogramma, Endlers, Dwarf Shrimp, and some slower Tetras make great tank mates.

19. Which fish should I avoid to keep with my Betta?

If it is a male Betta, keep it alone. Females can be kept in groups among themselves. This way, you avoid any problems. Never keep your Betta with aggressive and larger fish. Those fish can injure your fish. Also, avoid fish that will compete directly with Betta when feeding. Keep in mind that smaller fish, just as anything that fits in their mouth, will become food.

Bettas will not hesitate to bite fish with flashy and exuberant fins, such as Guppies. Therefore, always avoid using fish with these characteristics. Avoid large and aggressive fish like big cichlids. These types of fish can injure your Betta. And don't put fish that aren't compatible with your tank water.

20. Can I put plants in my Betta tank?

Try adding some live plants to your Betta tank. Aquatic plants help purify and oxygenate your aquarium water and provide a more beautiful and natural environment for your goldfish. Betta fish are found in tropical habitats filled with vegetation in the wild. Therefore, plants serve as a place to explore, obstacles to block their line of sight, and resting places to sleep at night.

Plants like Microsorum, Anubias, Amazon Sword, and Marimo Moss are excellent choices for this fish.

21. Can my Betta live in a bowl?

Bettas can even live in small bowls, but the quality of life is non-existent, to the point of even being considered animal cruelty.

If you have that image of a lone Betta living in a small aquarium, without further explanation, it died "out of nowhere." Better review this concept. Bettas are fish like any other. They deserve space to swim, equipment to maintain water quality, and other things that only a classic tropical aquarium can offer. Never keep your fish in small, unfiltered, or unheated spaces. Keep your tank clean, with maintenance and water quality tests up to date.

22. Which are the perfect tank and water parameters for my Betta?

First, get a Betta fish tank at least 5 gallons in volume; it should have a good length and width. Betta fish are tropical, meaning they need water with temperatures between 78 and 86 F. Therefore, it is crucial to have a heater to keep the water temperature stable. Keep the pH of the water in your Betta tank from slightly acidic to slightly alkaline, from 6.8 to 7.2. Ammonia, nitrite, and nitrate must always be

scaling 0.

Make use of many plants and natural decorations; in addition to bringing a more natural air to the tank, the fish will feel more comfortable.

You should always make use of a filter in your tank! This way, the filter will maintain water quality and oxygen levels for longer with less maintenance.

23. What is the best food for my Betta?

Bettas are considered carnivorous predatory fish and eat any animal that fits in their mouth.

In a natural environment, the fish feeds almost exclusively on insects, being an excellent predator, consuming a wide variety of insect species, both aquatic and terrestrial.

They have no problems eating and accepting different foods when kept in aquariums.

Keep a varied diet; offering commercial foods along with live and fresh foods, daphnias, earthworms, nauplii, tubifex, etc., will make your fish with much more striking colors.

Always offer an amount of food that the fish can consume in a short period. Always feed your Betta a rich and varied diet.

24. How often should I feed my Betta?

Due to the high metabolic

rate of Bettas, feeding it several times a day, in small amounts, is preferable.

Studies prove that food frequency is directly linked to the fish's quality of life, so we must, in addition to offering a balanced diet, provide small-sized foods numerous times a day. Remember, in this case, the smaller the size of the food, the better.

This rate also prevents leftover feed from being in the water, generating pollution, thus contributing to worsening the water quality of your tank.

25. How long can my Betta go without food?

This answer depends on some factors, but a Betta can go without food and remain healthy for less time when compared to other species.

We do not recommend leaving them without food

for more than three days.

26. How do I know if my Betta is sick?

Through observation, it is possible to tell when something is wrong with your Betta by the appearance and behavior of the fish.

In most cases, it is easy to identify if the fish is sick because physical changes can occur depending on the type of illness. Whether because of viruses, fungi, bacteria, or even parasites.

In cases where we have diseases due to bacteria, the main symptoms that your Betta will show are:
- Color loss;
- Fin rot;
- Wounds on the body;
- Difficulty breathing,
- Fish not eating.

In cases of fungal diseases, some of the manifestations can be:
- Different behavior;
- Whitish color around the eyes or mouth;
- Fish not eating.

Lastly, we have diseases caused by parasites. Some of the symptoms of Betta with parasites are:
- Fish is quieter, without many swimming movements;
- Body with a lot of mucus, which can even form a halo around the fish;
- Accelerated movement of the gills (difficult breathing);
- Small pale structures, usually shaped like a dot or comma (worms) on the body or gill of fish;
Controlling the environment, in this case, your tank's water, is the best way to prevent and cure diseases.

27. What are the most common diseases in Betta fish?

Commonly, we find some diseases that are more prevalent in Betta fish. They have different origins, such as parasites, bacteria, and fungi. Among the main external parasites (anchor worms, lice, and ticks), Ich (white spot disease) is the most prevalent, followed by Velvet Disease.
Regarding fungal and bacterial diseases, we can mention Saprolegniosis (winter fungus), Fin rot, and Cottonmouth disease. Constipation, Septicemia, and Dropsy are occurrences that we usually see and are directly linked to poor water quality.
Internal parasites and

viral infections are not so common in this species. It is possible to prevent all these diseases with simple actions. First, always clean the aquarium and provide everything the animal needs to live. Also, watch your betta fish as if they are sick; you will notice changes in their behavior or appearance. This way, we can identify the problems faster, and the treatment will be more effective. Lastly, make regular visits to the vet.

28. Why is my Betta fish spitting its food?

Fish from different species can put many types of food in their mouths and spit it out for several reasons.
However, the most straightforward answer is that your fish may not accept the food simply because they don't like it. Just like us, fish like to have different foods to eat.

29. Why doesn't my

Betta fish want to eat?
If your fish is not eating, there could be any number of reasons. The good news is that this fish not feeding symptom is as easy to spot as it is to remedy before it causes damage to your fish or tank.

The fact of not wanting to eat can indicate the lousy state of the general parameters of the water or be only the first symptom of some disease; detecting and resolving the problem quickly is vital when this happens.

30. Will my Betta fins grow back?
The good news is that bettas have a remarkable ability to regenerate their tails. We can see a full recovery of the fins and tail with proper treatment in very little time. Maintaining fish well-being and water

quality is essential to prevent the problem from reappearing.

31. How do I know if my Betta is bloated or just fat?

When the fish overeat, it may show a slightly distended abdomen, which is quite different from constipation or Dropsy bloating.

Suppose your Betta fish is constipated, this usually happens due to poor-quality food, and it is recommended that you act quickly.

Try to change the food, preferably using live food such as brine shrimp. Then, notice if the fish is defecating and deflating after changing the food.

The second reason that may be causing Betta fish to have a swollen belly is Dropsy, a hazardous condition, which means a bacterial infection already

in an advanced stage. The most evident symptom you can see in fish suffering from Dropsy is their abdomen showing a significant swelling. The term itself is used to describe swelling caused by fluid buildup. This fluid accumulation occurs in cavities and between tissues. As much as the swelling is usually located in the belly, this is not always the case.

In some situations, other symptoms are evident, such as bristly scales, swollen anus and eyes, pale gills, and stringy stools.

Dropsy is very common among fish and is identified as a symptom rather than an actual disease. A fish showing signs of Dropsy may suffer from various problems. It is easy to notice changes in behavior, such as the animal becoming quieter and lethargic, standing still at the bottom of the aquarium, or between decorations. In addition, they may remain close to the surface and appear to lack appetite.

32. How does Betta fish fight?

The first sign that the fish is ready to fight is the demonstration of its fully open fins (fin flare), lateral body movements, and open mouth.

That way, the fish looks bigger, thus frightening its

opponents.
Attacks are made through relentless chasing, biting, scratching, and tearing off other fish pieces.

33. What are these bubbles on the surface of my Betta tank?

These bubbles are the well-known bubble nest and are part of the breeding of Bettas.

The first time we see a betta fish making bubbles on the surface of the aquarium, it is common for us to be amazed, thinking that the fish has some disease or shortness of breath, but don't worry, this behavior is typical for an adult betta fish. It is part of the process of reproduction of the species.

When the male betta fish reaches adulthood and is healthy, he is ready to breed. Then he will start the process of building his bubble nest. This nest will be for him to put the fertilized eggs that he gets from the female partner.

The bubble nest is the way for the betta fish to show its sexual maturity. Although the bettas' reproduction process is incredible, putting your male together with a female is not an obligation. It is okay to clean the aquarium and dismantle the nest.

This behavior of the Betta fish is expected during the mating season and shows that the fish is in good health.

34. Why is my Betta staying in the bottom of the tank?

There are many reasons your betta fish is standing or lying on the bottom of the aquarium.
The Betta may be suffering from nitrate and nitrite poisoning, it may have some illness, it may just be the fish's temperament, something may have stressed it out, the temperature and aquarium may be inappropriate, or it may just be sleeping or resting. Some of these causes are entirely normal, while others may require a bit of your attention.
Several diseases can trigger this problem. Taking into account that the causes and solutions can be several, we recommend that you contact a veterinarian or specialist who will be able to help you.

35. Why is my Betta floating upside down?

While this is a not-so-common condition in Betta fish, it probably has something to do with the swim bladder. That is a little serious and, at the same time, quickly resolved.

Swim bladder diseases can be easily diagnosed as the fish affected by this disease will start swimming backward or randomly, so the belly will be located upwards. The consequence of swimming like this often is that the fish will continue hitting everything that crosses its path, as it doesn't have the same abilities to eat or keep the same balance.

Several diseases can trigger this problem. Taking into account that the causes and solutions can be several, we recommend that you contact a veterinarian or specialist who will be able to help you.

36. Why is my Betta jumping out of the tank?

Betta fish are natural jumpers. They use their jumps to move between different pools of water in the wild and hunt for food on the water's surface. If the jumps are recurrent, it can show that your Betta is bothered by something in the tank. For example, bettas can jump when stressed by poor water quality, have a parasite in their body, or are attacked by other fish. Ensure your aquarium has a tight lid, as these fish can escape through minor holes.

37. Why is my Betta fish hiding in the aquarium?

Having a fish hiding in the aquarium is not an alarm bell, as this is the typical behavior of many species. However, it can be a problem if it has happened suddenly or has associated symptoms, such as a fish that doesn't eat or stays at the bottom of the aquarium.

Fish often hide when they feel stressed by external factors or internal problems (illness). However, some species only hide when they are stressed.

The external stressors that can cause your fish to be hidden in the aquarium include aggression

from other fish, water conditions and quality, especially for new fish, and too bright lighting. Internal health factors include parasites, disease, and digestive problems.

Common Care Mistakes

1. About the myth of keeping Bettas in a small aquarium or bowl without equipment.

It is clear to anyone who has been in the aquarium hobby for a long time that most bettas live in tiny aquariums owned by first-time hobbyists.

I believe many people have never seen a Betta in an aquarium larger than 1 gallon. Well, this is one of this hobby's biggest injustices and myths.

The impact of a small aquarium on your fish's life can be much more significant than you might think. A fish living in a tiny aquarium will be much more stressed and likely be a very depressed animal.

All these factors significantly affect your fish's immunity, thus compromising your animal's health.

Like dirty aquariums, stress is one of the leading causes of disease and death in Betta fish. Concerning the size of the tank and the amount of time your Betta is living under such conditions, his immunity can be compromised entirely. Also, the smaller the aquarium, the more difficult it is to use necessary equipment such as filters and heaters. Smaller aquariums require persistent partial water changes to keep the water of good quality. Small aquariums are also more susceptible to sudden changes in pH and temperature, which significantly affect your pet's immunity. Therefore, having an aquarium that is too small only causes problems for your fish. If your Betta is sick, has swollen eyes or bellies, has a rotten or frayed tail, is lethargic, or has faded colors, one of the leading causes for this problem could be your fish tank. It is impossible to have a fully healthy betta in a tiny aquarium like the ones we see.

Carry out tests such as ammonia and pH in your tank. Only then will you know the efficiency of your filtration system.

2. Can I overfeed my Betta fish?

Bettas can be prone to obesity. In addition, other problems caused by overfeeding are digestive problems and the accumulation of food scraps in the aquarium. With this, the remains will end up at the bottom of the aquarium, where they are decomposed by bacteria, releasing ammonia. This toxic substance can even kill the fish. Therefore, be restrained and disciplined when feeding the fish.

3. Can I feed my Betta only live feed?

Yes, for sure, and they will love it and grow up super healthy; this is one of the "secrets" of Asian breeders.

The problem is that your fish will get spoiled and may no longer accept commercial food.

Filtration is one of the determining factors for the success of your aquarium. Classify filtration as the lung or heart of the aquarium. Through filtration, we will have clean, quality water, leaving it crystalline, odorless, and habitable for fish and plants of all kinds.

4. Betta fish must live alone.

This claim is nothing more than a myth. Despite being territorial, this swimmer does not necessarily need to live alone. However, before acquiring a tankmate, it is essential to know if he has a peaceful temperament and lives in the same temperature and pH conditions as the Betta fish.

Now, no problem if you insist on having more than one fish. Some species options are generally compatible with the Betta: Corydoras, Otos, Tanicts, Rasboras, and Loaches.

In this book, we covered the most common questions to successfully keep colorful and imponent Betta and an incredible Betta fish tank. Hopefully, you now have a better idea of what it is like to keep a Betta Fish as a pet.

As you can see, Bettas are incredibly hardy fish with stunning colors and curious behavior. If you like to keep fish that interact with you and exhibit a unique appearance, prepare your tank and go for the most incredible Betta!

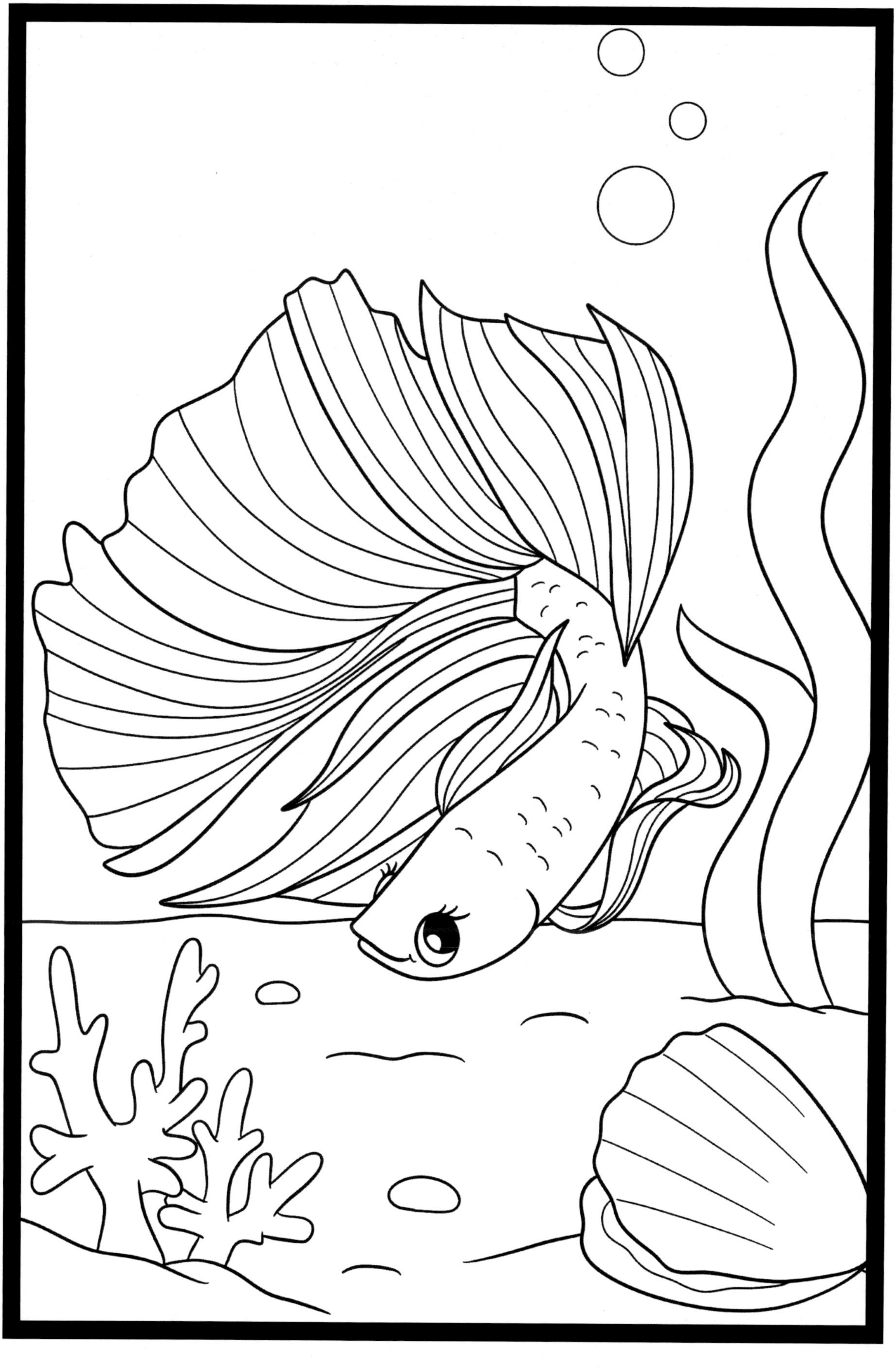

40 • FUN FACTS ABOUT BETTA FISH

Betta Fish Word Search

Find and circle the words.

A	S	F	M	N	S	I	A	M	E	S	E	M
F	D	A	O	O	T	C	X	Z	N	V	B	C
I	U	A	R	Y	R	P	L	K	J	G	F	R
G	A	Q	P	W	O	Q	Z	A	S	D	F	O
H	K	U	H	J	P	O	I	U	Y	T	R	W
T	C	A	R	N	I	V	O	R	O	U	S	N
I	A	W	X	D	C	F	G	V	B	C	X	T
N	P	E	O	I	A	Y	U	T	H	F	Z	A
G	A	G	F	I	L	T	E	R	S	Z	S	I
L	T	E	M	P	E	R	A	T	U	R	E	L

AQUA
TROPICAL
SIAMESE
FIGHTING
CROWNTAIL
MORPH
CARNIVOROUS
TEMPERATURE
FILTER

Solution at Page 45

Download Five Betta Fish Posters

Scan w/your Camera to Download!

A Message From The Author

Hello from Oliver and her mom! We're the creators of The World of Rare Pets series of books.

Our hope is that you and your loved ones enjoy each and every book we create. It's our mission to reduce impulsive buying of rare pets & educate children beforehand so that they know what it's like to keep a pet responsibly.

We are no big publishing house with tons of money to throw in marketing efforts, so the only way to spread the word about our books is you, our lovely customers. If you like our book, please consider giving us your **honest feedback with a review on Amazon.** When you post a review on Amazon it really makes a huge difference towards helping a small business like ours.

We sincerely appreciate your purchase and for supporting our small business.

References

Alton L.A., Portugal S.J., White C.R. (2012). Balancing the competing requirements of air-breathing and display behaviour during male-male interactions in Siamese fighting fish Betta splendens. Comparative Biochemistry and Physiology Part A: Molecular & Integrative Physiology 164(2), 363-367

Braddock J.C., Braddock Z.I. (1955). Aggressive behavior among females of the Siamese fighting fish, Betta splendens. Physiological Zoology 28, 152-172.

Braddock J.C., Braddock Z.I. (1959). The development of nesting behaviour in the Siamese fighting fish Betta splendens. Animal Behaviour 7, 222-232.

Bronstein P.M. (1982). Breeding, paternal behavior, and their interruption in Betta splendens. Animal Learning Behavior 10, 145-151.

Chalokpunrat, P. (1982). How to breed Siamese fighting fish. Aquaria 1, 57-59.

Chapman F.A., Fitz-Coy S.A. (1997). United States of America trade in ornamental fish. Journal of the World Aquaculture Society 28.

Choola, L. (1930). Some of observation on the breeding of fighting fish. Journal of Siam Society, Natural History Supplement 8, 91-97.

Clayton, F. L. & Hinde, R. A. (1968). The habituation and recovery of aggressive display in Betta splendens. Behaviour 30, 96-106.

FAWC (2009). Independent report. FAWC Report on Farm Animal Welfare in Great Britain: Past, Present and Future. FAWC advice to government and Animal welfare.

FitzGerald, G. J., Whoriskey, F. G., Morrissette, J. & Harding, M. (1992). Habitat scale, female cannibalism, and male reproductive success in threespine sticklebacks (Gasterosteus aculeatus). Behavioural Ecology 3, 141-147.

Goldstein R (2004). The Betta Handbook. Barrons educational series Inc., New York.

Gordon, M. & Axelrod, H. R. (1968). Siamese Fighting Fish. New Jersey: T. F. H. Publications.

Jaroensutasinee M., Jaroensutasinee K. (2001). Bubble nest habitat characteristics of wild Siamese fighting fish. Journal of Fish Biology 58, 1311-1319.

Kang C.K., Lee T.H. (2010). The Pharyngeal organ in the buccal cavity of the male Siamese fighting fish, betta splendens, supplies mucus for building bubble nests. Zoology Science 27, 861-866.

Liem K.F. (1963). The comparative osteology and phylogeny of the Anabantoidei (Teleostei, Pisces) 30. Illinois Biological Monographs 30, 1-149

Meejui O., Sukmanomon S., Na-Nakorn U. (2005). Allozyme revealed substantial genetic diversity between hatchery stocks of Siamese fighting fish, Betta splendens, in the province of Nakornpathom, Thailand. Aquaculture 250, 110-119.

Moore W.G. (1942). Field Studies on the oxygen requirements of certain freshwater fishes. Ecology 23, 319-329.

Oliveira, R. F., McGregor, P. K. & Latruffe, C. (1998). Know thine enemy: fighting fish gather information from observing conspecific interactions. Proceedings of Royal Society of London B 265, 1045-1049.

Pleeging, CCF, and Christel Moons. 2017. "Potential Welfare Issues of the Siamese Fighting Fish (Betta Splendens) at the Retailer and in the Hobbyist

Aquarium."Vlaams Diergeneeskundig Tijdschrift" 86 (4): 213-223.

Simpson M.J.A. (1968). The display of the Siamese fighting fish, Betta splendens. Animal Behavior Monographs 1, 1-74.

Smith H.M. (1945). Fresh Water Fishes of Siam. Smithsonian Libraries.

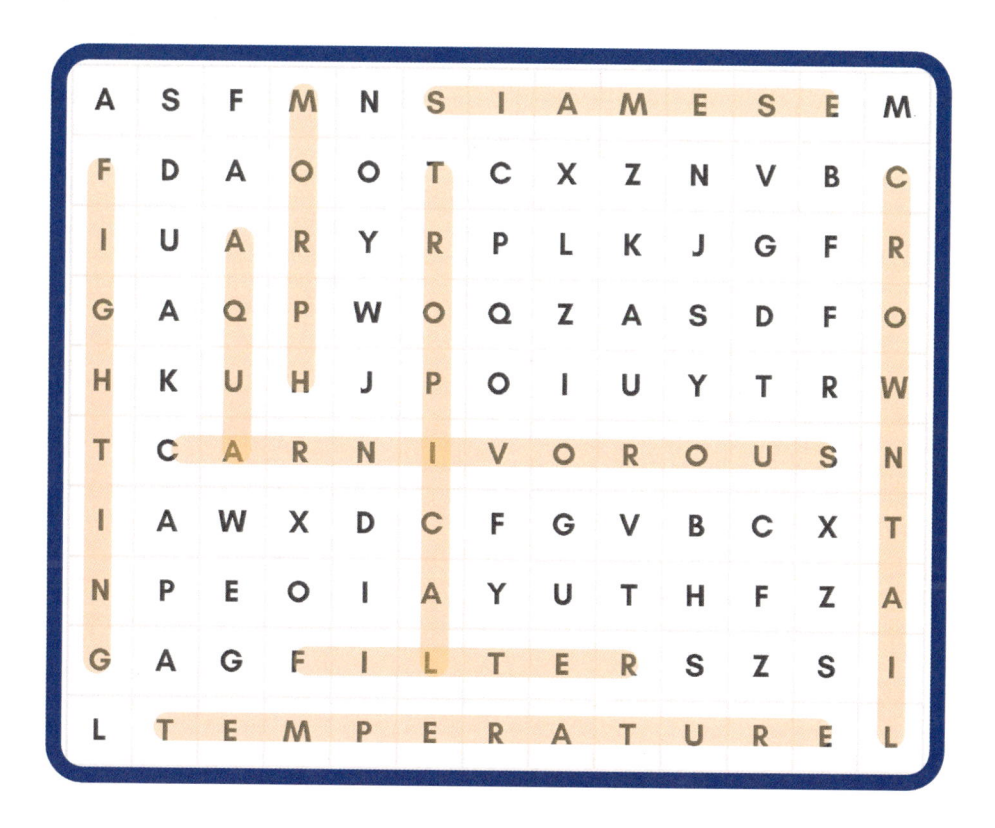

A	S	F	M	N	S	I	A	M	E	S	E	M
F	D	A	O	O	T	C	X	Z	N	V	B	C
I	U	A	R	Y	R	P	L	K	J	G	F	R
G	A	Q	P	W	O	Q	Z	A	S	D	F	O
H	K	U	H	J	P	O	I	U	Y	T	R	W
T	C	A	R	N	I	V	O	R	O	U	S	N
I	A	W	X	D	C	F	G	V	B	C	X	T
N	P	E	O	I	A	Y	U	T	H	F	Z	A
G	A	G	F	I	L	T	E	R	S	Z	S	I
L	T	E	M	P	E	R	A	T	U	R	E	L

AQUA FIGHTING CARNIVOROUS
TROPICAL CROWNTAIL TEMPERATURE
SIAMESE MORPH FILTER

Made in the USA
Monee, IL
17 September 2023